CIO Communication Skills Secrets

Tips And Techniques For CIOs To Use In Order To Become Better Communicators

"Practical, proven techniques that will help you to make your CIO career long and successful"

Dr. Jim Anderson

Published by:
Blue Elephant Consulting
Tampa, Florida

Copyright © 2013 by Dr. Jim Anderson

All rights reserved. No part of this book may be reproduced of transmitted in any form or by any means, electronic or mechanical, including photocopying, recording or by any information storage and retrieval system without written permission of the publisher, except for inclusion of brief quotations in a review.

Printed in the United States of America

Library of Congress Control Number: 2013921828

ISBN-13: 978-1494284411
ISBN-10: 1494284413

Warning – Disclaimer

The purpose of this book is to educate and entertain. This book does not promise or guarantee that anyone following the ideas, tips, suggestions, techniques or strategies will be successful. The author, publisher and distributor(s) shall have neither liability nor responsibility to anyone with respect to any loss or damage caused, or alleged to be caused, directly or indirectly by the information contained in this book.

Other Books By The Author

Product Management

- How To Have A Successful Product Manager Career: The Things That You Need To Be Doing TODAY In Order To Have A Successful Product Manager Career

- Product Manager Product Success: How to keep your product on track and make it become a success

- Communication Skills For Product Managers: The Communication Skills That Product Managers Need To Know How To Use In Order To Have A Successful Product

- Product Failure Lessons For Product Managers: Examples Of Products That Have Failed For Product Managers To Learn From

Public Speaking

- Secrets To Planning The Perfect Speech

- Secrets To Organizing The Perfect Speech: How to organize the best speech of your life!

- Secrets To Creating The Perfect Speech: How to create a speech that will make your message be remembered forever!

CIO Skills

- CIO Business Skills: How CIOs can work effectively with the rest of the company!

- Managing Your CIO Career: Steps That CIOs Have To Take In Order To Have A Long And Successful Career

IT Manager Skills

- IT Manager Budgeting Skills

- IT Manager Career Secrets: Tips And Techniques That IT Managers Can Use In Order To Have A Successful Career

Negotiating

- Preparing For Your Next Negotiation: What You Need To Do BEFORE A Negotiation Starts In Order To Get The Best Possible Deal

- How To Open Your Next Negotiation: How To Start A Negotiation In Order To Get The Best Possible Outcome

Miscellaneous

- Power Distribution Unit (PDU) Secrets: What Everyone Who Works In A Data Center Needs To Know!

- Making The Jump: How To Land Your Dream Job When You Get Out Of College!

Acknowledgements

Any book like this one is the result of years of real-world work experience. In my over 25 years of working for 7 different firms, I have met countless fantastic people and I've been mentored by some truly exceptional ones. Although I've probably forgotten some of the people who made me the person that I am today, here is my attempt to finally give them the recognition that they so truly deserve:

- Thomas P. Anderson
- Art Puett
- Bobbi Marshall
- Bob Boggs

Dr. Jim Anderson

This book is dedicated to my wife Lori. None of this would have been possible without her love and support.

Thanks for the best 21 years of my life (so far)...!

Speaking.   Negotiating.   Managing.   Marketing.

Table Of Contents

THE MOST EFFECTIVE CIOS ARE THE ONES WHO COMMUNICATE THE BEST 8

ABOUT THE AUTHOR 10

CHAPTER 1: SOFT WORK IN HARD TIMES 15

CHAPTER 2: WHEN GIVING IT INFORMATION, MORE IS BETTER 18

CHAPTER 3: FORGOTTEN IT SKILLS: HOW TO ASK QUESTIONS 21

CHAPTER 4: IRAN'S TWITTER REVOLUTION HOLDS LESSONS FOR CIOS 24

CHAPTER 5: CIOS ASK THE QUESTION: IS TWITTER A FRIEND OR A FOE? 28

CHAPTER 6: SHOULD A CIO BOTHER WITH THAT ITIL STUFF? 32

CHAPTER 7: HEY CIO: WOULD YOU LIKE A WIKI? 36

CHAPTER 8: WHY EVERY FUTURE CIO SHOULD BE "TWEETING" (THIS MEANS YOU) 39

CHAPTER 9: 3 SKILLS THAT MOST CIOS ARE MISSING 44

CHAPTER 10: HEY CIO, ARE YOU SENDING THE WRONG SIGNALS? ... 48

CHAPTER 11: WHAT CIOS CAN LEARN FROM GM ABOUT ELIMINATING RED TAPE 52

CHAPTER 12: HOW CIOS WORK WITH THEIR BOARD OF DIRECTORS 56

The Most Effective CIOs Are The Ones Who Communicate The Best

Isn't technology a wonderful thing? As CIO you are in charge of one of the most technologically sophisticated parts of the company. It's very easy to fill your days dealing with issues regarding servers, networks, routers, switches, firewalls, etc. However, it turns out that if you do this, then you'll be overlooking one of the most important tasks that a CIO needs to accomplish: communication.

Keeping all of the moving parts that an IT department has in alignment is a challenging task. The good news is that you don't have to do it all – that's what the rest of the IT department is there for. However, you do need to clearly communicate to everyone both inside and outside of the IT department what you want to have done. This is going to require you to have good communication skills.

Communication skills include knowing how to ask good questions, understanding how to use social media tools like Twitter, and realizing how to apply ITIL to your IT department. All of this stuff takes time to both learn and do.

This book has been written in order to show you what you need to be doing in order to get your message out. In order to get the rest of the company to line up behind you and do what you need them to do, they first have to hear and understand your message. I'm going to show you many different ways that you can connect with the people who have to hear your message and how you can make your requests "stick" with them.

It is my hope that after having read this book you will be aware of how to clearly communicate with not only your IT department, but also with the rest of the company. Do this correctly and your CIO career will last a long time...!

For more information on what it takes to be a great CIO, check out my blog, The Accidental Successful CIO, at:

www.TheAccidentalSuccessfulCIO.com

Good luck!

- Dr. Jim Anderson

About The Author

I must confess that I never set out to be a CIO. When I went to school, I studied Computer Science and thought that I'd get a nice job programming and that would be that. Well, at least part of that plan worked out!

My first job was working for Boeing on their F/A-18 fighter jet program. I spent my days programming fighter jet software in assembly language and I loved it. The U.S. government decided to save some money and went looking for other countries to sell this plane to. This put me into an unfamiliar role: I started to meet with foreign military officials and I ended up having to manage groups of engineers who were working on international projects.

Time moved on and so did I. I found myself working for Siemens, the big German telecommunications company. They were making phone switches and selling them to the seven U.S. phone companies. The problem was that the switches were too complicated. Customers couldn't tell the difference between one complicated phone switch from another complicated phone switch. Once again I found myself working with the sales and marketing teams to find ways to make the great technology that the engineers had developed understandable to both internal and external customers.

I've spent over 25 years working as an senior IT professional for both big companies and startups. This has given me an opportunity to learn what it takes to manage and IT department in ways that allow it to maximize its output while becoming a valuable part of the overall company.

I now live in Tampa Florida where I spend my time managing my consulting business, Blue Elephant Consulting, teaching college courses at the University of South Florida, and traveling to work with companies like yours to share the knowledge that I have about how to create and manage successful IT departments.

I'm always available to answer questions and I can be reached at:

Dr. Jim Anderson
Blue Elephant Consulting
Email: jim@BlueElephantConsulting.com
Facebook: http://goo.gl/1TVoK
Web: http://www.BlueElephantConsulting.com/

"Unforgettable communication skills that will set your ideas free..."

Create IT Departments That Are Productive And A Valuable Asset To The Rest Of The Company !

Dr. Jim Anderson is available to provide training and coaching on the topics that are the most important to people who have to manage IT departments: how can I build a productive IT department (and keep it together) while at the same time providing the rest of the company with the IT services that they need?

Dr. Anderson believes that in order to both learn and remember what he says, speakers need to laugh. Each one of his speeches is full of fun and humor so that what he says "sticks" with everyone.

Dr. Anderson's CIO SkillsTraining Includes:

1. How to identify and attract the right type of IT workers to your IT department.
2. How to build relationships with the company's senior management in order to get the support that you need?
3. How to stay on top of changing technology and security issues so that you never get surprised?

Dr. Jim Anderson works with over 100 customers per year. To invite Dr. Anderson to work with you, contact him at:

Phone: 813-418-6970 or
Email: jim@BlueElephantConsulting.com

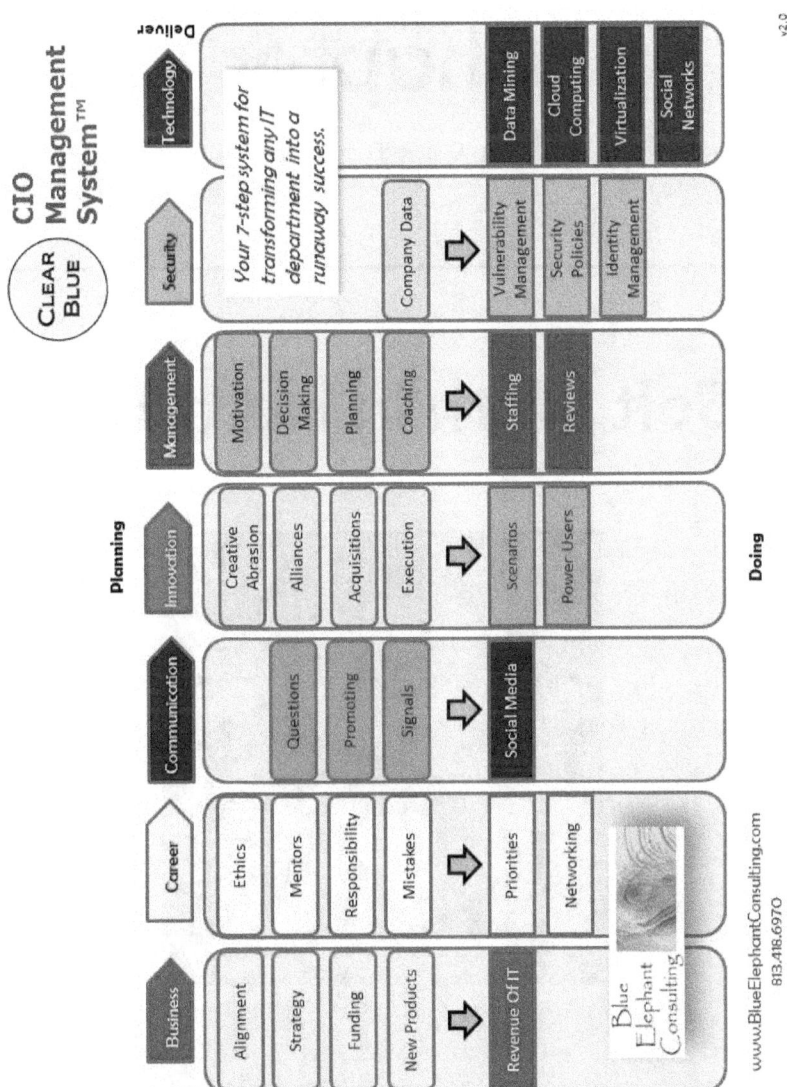

The Clear Blue CIO Management System™ has been created to provide CIOs and senior IT managers with a clear roadmap for how to manage an IT department. This system shows CIOs what needs to be done and in what order to do it.

Chapter 1

Soft Work In Hard Times

Chapter 1: Soft Work In Hard Times

It would appear as though the U.S. economy is starting to pull out of its recent downturn; however, for those of us in the IT industry, this should serve as yet another wake-up call for both ourselves and our teams: technical skills alone are not going to cut it anymore.

Generally when I say that, heads start to nod. However, nobody seems to know the answer to the very next question: so what to do about it? For IT departments to transform themselves from where they are today to where they need to be tomorrow, there are a whole new set of skills that everyone needs to learn and the quicker, the better. You've heard this phrase before and you're going to hear it from me one more time: **soft skills**.

More head nodding should be occurring right now. The big question is what soft skills do IT departments need to get good at? There are lots of these skills, but I believe that for IT they can be placed into five groups:

1. **Negotiation Skills**: proving once again that it's not what you know, but what you know how to get done that is most valuable to the company. As IT departments start to rely on outside vendors more and more, the ability to properly negotiate agreements becomes a must have skill.

2. **Communication Skills**: being the best technical worker is of almost no value to the company if you can't communicate what you are working on and the challenges that you are facing. Putting together a 100+ slide PowerPoint deck does not mean that you can communicate. Using a three slide PowerPoint deck to clearly communicate your point does.

3. **Your Business Knowledge**: knowing what your business does, how it does it, and why it does it has become critical knowledge for all IT workers. Ultimately the goal is to align what IT does with where the company wants to go and knowing what the business side of the house is trying to do is the key to being able to do this.

4. **Team Motivation Skills**: knowing how to get a group of people to work together towards a shared goal has always been important and now it is a required skill. Everybody is understaffed and overworked. Having the ability to cut through all of the clutter and get folks to accomplish an objective makes you worth your weight in gold to the company.

5. **IT Product Management Skills**: even if everyone is not a product manager, having the basic product management skills of scheduling, planning, and coordinating are critical to making sure that the project that you are working on is a success. Once the IT department is aligned with the rest of the business, missing delivery dates can have significant impacts on the company's bottom line.

These are my picks for the top five must-have IT department soft skills, what do you think – got any to add to the list?

Chapter 2

When Giving IT Information, More Is Better

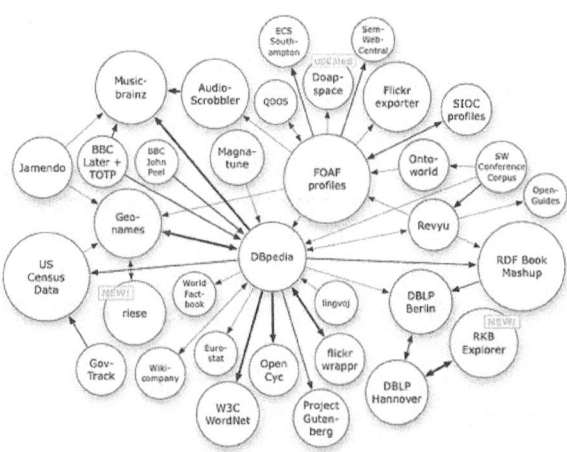

Chapter 2: When Giving IT Information, More Is Better

So just what is the job of an IT department once you get past the keeping the network up and applications running stuff? I think that we can all agree that it must have something to do with **the company's data**, but exactly what does that mean?

Ranjay Gulati, James Oldroyd, and Phanish Puranam are three researchers who have been studying this problem and they've made some interesting discoveries. They realize that IT is the source for countless reports – our job is to turn data into information that the company can take action on.

However, they've discovered that it can be just as important that we share with the rest of the company **HOW** we've come to know something as well as **WHAT** we know.

Now this is the tricky part: IT needs to find ways to tell our audience the answers to their questions AND we need to tell them **how we got the data** and what, if any, strengths and weakness there are with that data.

If you want to get all fancy about this the word to use would be that we need to provide "**metadata**" with our reports. A good example of this would come from the Royal Bank of Canada.

A few years ago the bank implemented a system that when a customer was overdrawn on a check, the system would do some credit / overdraft history checking in order to determine if a **courtesy overdraft** should be granted.

The information on the system and the data that it used was distributed in the bank and an ATM product manager happened to read it. He realized that a similar system could be created to provide **overdrafts for ATM customers**. The bank spent about

$100,000 to implement this new service and since then has made millions off of it.

Allowing staff to not only see the output of an IT department, but also the **information on the data that was used to create that output** allows more people to find ways to reapply the data in ways that you may have never thought of.

Chapter 3

Forgotten IT Skills: How To Ask Questions

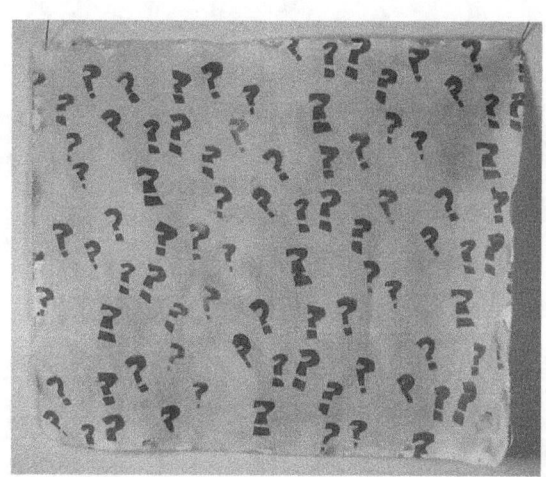

Chapter 3: Forgotten IT Skills: How To Ask Questions

It's easy to get caught up in all of the servers, routers, applications, and firewalls that make up a modern IT environment. After a while we tend to start thinking that the path to our next great IT insight must lie somewhere in this jungle of IT "stuff". And that is where you'd be **wrong**!

Ranjay Gulati, James Oldroyd, and Phanish Puranam are three researchers who have been studying this problem and they've made some interesting discoveries. They've come to realize that if IT folks like us want to help our firms uncover ideas for new products or services, then we may have to rediscover the ancient art of **asking the right questions**.

I will confess to being just as guilty of this as everyone else. In order to be **more productive**, I try to ask pointed questions that get right to the (what else) point. The researchers are saying that this is exactly the wrong thing to be doing.

What they are saying is that more often than not other parts of the company will have information and data that can help us uncover new products and solutions if only we know how to ask for it. If we re-train ourselves to start asking **broad questions**, then we will start to get exposed to more types of information.

An example of this comes from the folks at **Harrah's**. The IT department was helping out with a project that was designed to find out what hotels were in need of expansion. They asked the question "**What is the demand for our hotel rooms?**" Note what they didn't ask: "What is our occupancy rate?" The broad way that the question was asked allowed both the occupancy rate and the number of people unable to book a room because of the hotel being full or because they were unwilling to pay the room rate to be counted. A much different answer!

Getting IT staff to start asking broad questions is not easy. They will be giving up some efficiency, but **the rewards can be great**.

Chapter 4

Iran's Twitter Revolution Holds Lessons For CIOs

Chapter 4: Iran's Twitter Revolution Holds Lessons For CIOs

Politics is a fascinating subject and I'm sure that we all have our own opinions about the events that unfolded over in Iran regarding their elections. However, this chapter isn't about the elections or who won. Rather it's about the **amazing flow of information** that happened even in a heavily restricted / controlled environment. We live in the 21st Century and this story holds many lessons for modern CIOs...

What Does An Election In Iran Have To Do With Twitter?

Noam Cohen over at the New York Times has taken a look at how information has flowed since the unrest began. In all honesty, "**twitter revolution**" is probably an overstatement. Web sites, text messages, and simple person-to-person conversation probably did a better job of spreading news than Twitter did. However, Twitter did do an amazing job of getting information OUT of the country.

Remember that Twitter is only three years old. Its impact is much greater than its age would lead a CIO to believe. Although you might not be dealing with a disputed election, Twitter could **play a big role** in your company's future.

What Twitter Means To Your Firm

There will be times in the future that your senior management (CEO, Chairman, etc.) will want to control what information is released about your firm and they would like to have some control over what people are saying about your company. Twitter opens up a **whole new channel** for people to talk about your firm. Here are six lessons that the Iranian elections have taught all of us about this powerful new communication tool:

- **Twitter Really Can't Be Stopped**: Twitter messages ("tweets") are really a form of one-to-many communications. There is no centralized site that can be shut down or forced to remove information by court order. There is no stopping this beast.

- **There Is Power In Numbers**: A single tweet probably doesn't mean much. A couple of tweets won't attract attention. However, a series of tweets about the same subject will start to create an ecosystem about an event or a viewpoint. This can attract attention and start to generate more conversations.

- **Buyer Beware**: Remember, on the Internet nobody knows that you are a dog (a saying from the early years of the Internet). Since the people participating in Twitter have no real identity, you really can't trust what they are saying until it has been verified.

- **Home Of Bad Information**: There are probably people trying to communicate truths using Twitter, but there are probably also people who are trying to spread lies using Twitter. Whether it's to drive your stock price down (or up) or prevent / encourage a takeover, all sorts of people will use Twitter to spread completely made-up stories.

- **Twitter People Use Twitter**: CIOs always have to keep in mind that the people using Twitter are generally tech savvy folks who are online a lot. This does not necessarily represent the public at large.

- **Twitter Is Connected To The Media**: The popular media "gets" Twitter and they are listening in order to get leads on new stories and dig up sources. This means that almost any storyteller now has a potential direct line to a major media outlet.

Final Thoughts

Twitter is yet one more way for people to communicate. It takes a little getting used to for most of us as we struggle to understand why anyone would take the time to send 140 character messages to communicate when we have so many other tools that we can use. However Twitter (and all of its variants) **are here to stay**.

CIOs need to adapt to this new world. When future events affect your company (disasters, mergers, takeovers, product issues, etc.) Twitter will probably **play a role** in how information gets out to the world at large. Developing a communication strategy that includes Twitter is a critical CIO responsibility. Addressing this issue this will mean that CIOs will have **found a way** to apply IT to enable the rest of the company to grow quicker, move faster, and do more.

Chapter 5

CIOs Ask The Question: Is Twitter A Friend Or A Foe?

Chapter 5: CIOs Ask The Question: Is Twitter A Friend Or A Foe?

When you become CIO you will have a number of tools available to you that CIOs never had in the past. #1 on this list is, of course, Twitter. However, wait a minute, **is this a good thing or a bad thing?** Sounds like you need to figure this out before you become CIO and make a mistake...

What Does Twitter Mean To A CIO?

Ultimately everything that a CIO does needs to be about finding ways to **create more business for the company**. That brings up the interesting question about Twitter: is this a good place for the company to be looking for customers?

While that question may currently have no clear answer, the one thing that nobody can argue with is the simple fact that **Twitter is currently growing like a weed**. Although different people come up with different numbers, everyone agrees that Twitter currently has between 18 – 23 million users. No matter how you slice it, that's a lot of your potential customers!

So why are people using this service that restricts you to sending short 140 character bursts of text messages? A recent survey of Twitter users revealed that 42% of Twitter users use it to communicate ("tweet") in order to **connect with friends**. 14% do it in order to have more interaction and access to their favorite companies, and 13% are doing it in order to be able to connect with service providers.

While this all sounds wonderful, it turns out that most of the companies that are already using Twitter **really have no idea how to make the most of this new resource**. It's almost like when the Internet first showed up – everyone is once again going through a learning process.

Ways That A CIO Can Use Twitter

As a CIO, just saying "we're going to use Twitter" is not enough, you need to come up with **a concrete plan** for how your firm can use Twitter in order to have a direct impact on developing more sales leads or even generating revenue. The good news here is that as you develop a Twitter plan for your company, you can be using Twitter because as many companies have found out there is very little risk to using this tool.

The computer company Dell is a clear leader in the field of companies that have found a way to maximize the value of Twitter. They have **generated $3M from their Twitter activities** since 2007. What Dell has been doing is using Twitter to post coupons and spread the word about new Dell products.

Other firms that are using Twitter view it as **being an amplifier** for their other marketing activities. This allows them to extend their reach and get more bang for their marketing buck.

There appears to be **two different paths for a company to follow** when they are using Twitter. One is to use it as another way to communicate what the corporate voice is saying. The other is to use it as a means to create a personal bond with their potential customers. Both ways work, you just need to make up your mind, pick one, and stick with it.

What All This Means For You

CIOs will always be facing the challenge of evaluating and deciding **if a new tool should be used by the company**. The sudden arrival and the overnight popularity of Twitter is a clear example of such a CIO opportunity.

Twitter has been adopted by a huge number of users who probably include both your existing and potential customers.

It's clear that the real question isn't IF you should use Twitter, but rather **HOW** you should use it going forward.

Coming up with **a clear Twitter strategy** should be your first step: are you simply going to amplify what you are already telling your customers or are you going to try to connect with them on a deeper level? Once you've made this decision, you'll have to devote the IT resources to making it happen on a consistent basis. Nobody ever said that being CIO was going to be easy, but maybe this will give you something to tweet about...

Chapter 6

Should A CIO Bother With That ITIL Stuff?

Johnson & Johnson
Family of Companies

Chapter 6: Should A CIO Bother With That ITIL Stuff?

Johnson & Johnson Had A Problem

I'm sure that when you picture yourself becoming a CIO in the future you see yourself sitting at the corporate strategy table with the CEO using your deep understanding of IT to help the company move faster and do more. Umm, one problem with that vision – you're not going to make it to the big table if you don't solve the problem of run-away IT costs.

Johnson & Johnson's CIO had this very same problem and she tackled it using the ITIL framework. Maybe this would be a good time to look into that ITIL thing...

Just What Is the ITIL?

You've probably heard about the IT Infrastructure Library (ITIL); however, do you really understand what it is? First off, it's a old (10 years is old by IT standards) set of best practice guidelines for how to do IT service management.

It was originally developed by the U.K. government in order to help them do a better job of modeling their outsourced IT projects. It's quite popular in European IT shops and is only now starting to pick up steam in the U.S.

What makes the ITIL so attractive is that it allows a CIO to run the IT department like a business. This is exactly what Johnson & Johnson's CIO was looking for back in 2001.

J&J was going gang-busters from a business point-of-view; however, their IT costs were going through the roof – they were going up by over 10% every year.

J&J had previously tried the old stand-by CIO trick of pulling together IT operations from all around the sprawling company into a single centralized organization in order to get on top of their costs. However, even though now they knew where the money was going, they still were seeing out-of-control growth on infrastructure tasks. Something had to be done!

J&J's CIO decided to implement a program based on the ITIL. Now mind you, this is not some silver-bullet magic cure-all.

Instead, the ITIL can help with specific parts of running an IT shop. Specifically if you go about implementing ITIL correctly, your IT department can boost the quality of service that it is providing to the rest of the company.

J&J's IT department was able to use ITIL to decrease how long it took to resolve problems. This in turn resulted in J&J's systems having more uptime and therefore allowing more work to be done quicker. Needless to say, end users were very happy about this.

Sure happy customers are nice, but what about the money? J&J says that if you count both cost savings and costs that they were able to avoid, then starting in 2005 they believe that they've been able to save at least $30M a year by implementing ITIL.

Why Did This Solution Work

ITIL is not the only way to standardize the way that a CIO runs his / her IT department. Other methods include the Capability Maturity Model (CMM), Control Objectives for Information and Related Technology (COBIT), Six Sigma, and Lean Manufacturing. However, ITIL has been around the longest and it has been shown to work.

Taking the ITIL path was the right choice for J&J for a number of reasons. Not the least of which was it provided J&J's CIO with a way to both quantify and measure the quality of the service that J&J's IT department was delivering. Who was the wise man who said "If you can't measure it, you can't improve it"?

What All Of This Means For You

When you become CIO you'll be facing the same twin set of conditions that can keep you from doing all of that strategic stuff that you want to be doing: rising IT costs and ever increasing user demands for more service. You are going to have to deal with this issue and do it quickly.

ITIL is not a new "flavor of the day" approach to solving the challenges that an IT department faces. In fact, it's a rather old approach. However, if you're willing to make the investment in time and energy that it can take, ITIL just might be the solution that you are looking for.

Knowing that there is a solution framework out there that works is what allows most CIOs to be able to sleep at night. Actually implementing a solution and saving the company, well that's a job that will be waiting for you when you become the CIO.

Chapter 7

Hey CIO: Would You Like A Wiki?

Chapter 7: Hey CIO: Would You Like A Wiki?

One of the biggest challenges that you are going to be facing when you become a CIO is managing an IT workforce that is made up of multiple generations. Each has its own set of views and skills, and yet you have to somehow come up with ways that they can work together. How hard could that be?

Can't We All Just Work Together?

An IT department is made up a whole bunch of different types of workers. The reason that you'll have such a challenge in getting them to work together is that they all see the world differently.

In order for your IT department to be successful, they are going to have to be able to successfully complete large IT projects. The secret to doing this type of work well is to engage in what the experts call "task sharing". This is no more complicated than taking a single large task and breaking it up into a series of smaller tasks.

IT teams that can do this have the ability to solve very large problems by working together. The ones who can't are the ones who exceed schedules and blow through budgets.

Welcome To The World Of Wikinomics

The term "wikinomics" was coined by Don Tapscott & Anthony Williams in their book "**Wikinomics: How Mass Collaboration Changes Everything**". They point out that for the first time ever, technology, demographics, and global economics have come together to make change and innovation easier than ever.

The use of Internet based tools like wikis finally has provided CIOs with the tools that they need in order to get their IT teams to do the one thing that will make them more successful: exchange information. No matter what generation a given worker is, the use of web-based communication tools is the common factor that will allow them to both send and receive the information that they will need to do better work

What All Of This Means For You

As CIO you will be faced with many challenges. Potentially the greatest of these will be finding a way to get your entire IT team to work together as a single smooth flowing unit.

The arrival of web based collaboration tools such as wikis may be the silver bullet that you need. All of a sudden it has become very easy for everyone in an IT department to both send and receive knowledge.

Just having the tools to exchange information is not enough. As CIO you are going to have to find ways to motivate your teams to use the tools that are available. That's why being a CIO is such a tough job!

Chapter 8

Why Every Future CIO Should Be "Tweeting" (This Means You)

Chapter 8: Why Every Future CIO Should Be "Tweeting" (This Means You)

Will these Internet crazes never end? Just in case you've been living under a rock someplace and haven't heard about the "Twitter" revolution, guess what: it's arrived and this time around as a CIO wanta-be you should be an active participant.

Just What Is This Twitter Thing?

If you're already "tweeting" every day, you can skip this part! In a nutshell, Twitter is sorta like the Citizen Band radios of the mid to late 1970s. Once you set up a Twitter account, you can either use the Twitter web page or download and install one of countless Twitter mobile phone apps to send out short messages telling the world what you are doing at any given point-in-time.

The key word here is "short" – a Twitter message (a "tweet" to those of us in the know), is limited to no more than 140 characters. Clearly we're not talking about sending out emails here.

Just to round out our comparison of Twitter to CBs, with a CB you needed to be on a certain radio channel if you wanted to hear what someone was saying. In the world of Twitter you need to be "following" someone if you want to be able to receive and read their tweets.

Why Should A CIO Care About This Twitter Thing?

So outside of being the latest Internet craze, why should someone who is interested in becoming a CIO spend any time looking into this whole Twitter thing? It turns out that there are three reasons: communication skills, info, and networking.

One of the most important and challenging things that a CIO does is to communicate with others. Although what you want to say may be clear in your head, actually getting the words on paper (or a screen) that will make it clear in your IT staff's heads is a completely different matter.

Twitter's limitation on how much information that you can pack into a single message, 140 characters, is both a curse and a blessing. It's a curse for those of us (myself included) who are very verbose and who will use two words when one would do just fine.

It's a blessing in that if you want to clearly communicate an idea in just 140 characters then you're going to have to do a great deal of self-editing. You're going to end up throwing away all of that fancy prose that you use and boiling your tweets down to just the core essence of what you want to say.

This is exactly what you should be doing when you are communicating with your team – getting rid of the fluff and just leaving the good stuff. By getting involved in the world of Twitter and actually spending time hand crafting your tweets, you'll refine your skills in this area. Sure, you could pay an expensive assistant help you refine your every communication, but it sure is cheaper to spend time on Twitter and learn to do it yourself.

Say Hello To Info

A nice side benefit to becoming active in the world of Twitter is that you'll grow a community of people who choose to follow you. This collection of people who may see every tweet that you send out are an incredibly valuable resource.

Staying on top of the world of IT is not an easy thing to do. Finding the information that you need and running what you are going to say by interested people are critical things that you need to do.

Your Twitter followers are the perfect source for information source recommendations as well as being able to provide quick feedback on just about anything you want to run by them. Even if you get something wrong, you won't embarrass yourself in front of your IT team.

It's All About Followers

Finally, networking is something that every CIO should be doing, but none of us ever seems to have enough time to do well . Sure you'll have a CIO job eventually, but what job will you have after that one? You always need to be working to build your network and Twitter is a great tool for doing this.

The more followers that you have in Twitter, the better your ability to get the word out about the great work that you are doing as a CIO. No, not every one of your followers will care about the problems that you are solving (it's a global service after all), but they sure will be able to pass the word on about all of your skills and experience and you'd be amazed at how powerful a force this can be.

What All Of This Means For You

It's starting to look as though the Internet tool called Twitter is here to stay. As more and more people sign up and start to "tweet", this is starting to become a genuine communication tool.

CIOs and future CIOs need to dive right in and start to use Twitter. The benefits are three-fold: using Twitter teaches CIOs how to concisely express their thoughts, it provides a new way to gather information and test ideas, and finally it is a great way to do professional networking.

All new things can be a bit intimidating at first. CB radios had their own lingo and user community when they first appeared. Don't be nervous about using Twitter, get started and find out just how eloquent you can be in just 140 characters!

Chapter 9

3 Skills That Most CIOs Are Missing

Chapter 9: 3 Skills That Most CIOs Are Missing

I'm guessing that you wouldn't go to work naked. Then why-oh-why are you thinking about becoming a CIO when you don't have all of the skills that you'll need to do the job correctly?

I'm not sure if this is going to make you feel any better, but it turns out that most CIOs are showing up for work only partially dressed when you consider **what skills they are missing**. Maybe we'd better have a talk about this...

Can You Communicate?

All too often, IT folks assume that good communication skills mean that you have the ability to get up in front of a group of people and **deliver a speech** without bursting into flames. Yes, this is good skill to have, but a CIO has to have more.

Remember, communication is **a two-way street** and not only does a CIO need to be able to tell others what to do, but you are also going to have to be able to listen to what others are telling you.

No, we're not talking about having the ability to sit there and listen when someone else is talking to you while you are just waiting for them to pause so that you can start talking again. Instead, a CIO needs to be able to listen, process what has been said, and then **ask good, pointed questions** that will help get to the bottom of any discussion.

Just to round things out, a CIO also needs to have the communication skills that will allow them to **"close" a discussion**. This is when you ask a final question and then have the strength to keep your mouth closed and allow the other person to provide an answer. This is how you wrap things up cleanly.

Promote, Promote, Promote!

All too often CIOs seem to have a "build it and they will come" sort of attitude. They believe that if both the IT department and, by extension, they do a good job then the rest of the company will realize it and **their value to the company will increase**. Sorry, it doesn't work that way.

What CIOs need to be doing is **constantly promoting** both themselves and the IT department. Now you have to be careful here, note that I didn't say "bragging". The difference is subtle, but important.

One way that a CIO can show the value of both his position as well as the IT department is to become the **thought leader** on all things technical. By researching new technologies and then taking the time to educate the rest of the company about what they mean and how they can be used by the business in order to be more successful, both the CIO and the IT department will become recognized as a valuable resource.

Make A Friend (or Two)

Within the world of IT, there is often **a "loner" attitude** that many of us hold: I can do it all by myself. When you become CIO, you need to stop thinking this way and start making as many contacts as you can.

A CIO is only as strong as his / her network and that means taking the time to **develop real relationships** with as many people as possible. Not all CIOs have this skill.

What All Of This Means For You

If you really want to become the CIO, **you've got some work to do**. There are a set of skills that you'll need to have developed before your big day comes.

In order to remain a CIO once you get there, you're going to have to have the ability to be **a good two-way communicator**. You'll have to learn to spend your time tirelessly promoting both the IT department and your value to the company. Finally, you are going to have to get good at that critical skill: networking.

None of these three skills are impossible to do. However, the key to being a successful CIO is to get good at **doing all three at the same time**...!

Chapter 10

Hey CIO, Are You Sending The Wrong Signals?

Chapter 10: Hey CIO, Are You Sending The Wrong Signals?

No matter if you are already a CIO or simply hope to become one someday, you are going to want to become a success. Just because you are the CIO, **does not guarantee that you'll be a success** – it seems to take something else, something extra. It turns out that social signals are what determine how successful a CIO will be. Do you know what signals you are sending out?

Welcome To The World Of "Honest Signals"

Dr. Alex Pentland at MIT has been studying **the social cues that we transmit to others**. What he's discovered is that we communicate with others using much more than words. What we are trying to communicate comes across in our gestures, expressions, and the tone that we use.

Dr. Pentland's research has gone one step further. What he's uncovered is that **we have a set of non-verbal cues**, what he calls "honest signals" that do more than just communicate from us to another person. They actually cause a change in the person that we are communicating with. In other words, what we are trying to get across "rubs off" on the person that we're interacting with.

We've all seen this before. If we encounter someone who is very excited and outgoing, then we'll become excited just by talking with them. Likewise, if we bump into someone who is having the worst day of their life, then we'll be down and glum after we talk with them.

Why Do Some CIOs Succeed And Others Don't?

Great, so now you've just found out that as CIO you are going to be **"leaking" information** through a bunch of non-verbal cues. That's a bummer, but does it really matter – I mean you've got your technical act together and you believe that you know how to run an IT department, right?

It turns out that the non-verbal cues that you are giving off **do matter**. What the researchers have found through study is that the more successful CIOs are also the ones who are more energetic.

What this means is that the CIOs who are going to both last in their roles and be successful **display a set of common traits**. These include talking to others more while at the same time taking the time to listen to them. More of their day is spent engaging in face-to-face discussions. They are better at working with other people and they can both pick up signals from others, get them to talk more, and get them to be more outgoing overall.

What the researchers have found is that your **attitude and the positive energy that you give off** play a key role in your eventual success. They've found that spending more face time with the people with whom you work is 2.5 times more important than gaining access to additional sources of information.

What All Of This Means For You

In order for a CIO to be successful, it's going to take a lot more than just having good technical knowledge. Researchers who study human dynamics have discovered what they call **"honest signals"** which can have a dramatic impact on your success.

These signals cause **changes in the people who receive them**. This means that in order to be successful as a CIO you need to be broadcasting the right signals. If not, then no matter how good your CIO skills are, you won't be successful.

The good news is that once you know that honest signals exist and which ones are the ones that you want to be broadcasting, then **you can focus on what you are transmitting**. Awareness of the impact that you have on the people that you are meeting is the key to a CIO's long-term career success…

Chapter 11

What CIOs Can Learn From GM About Eliminating Red Tape

Chapter 11: What CIOs Can Learn From GM About Eliminating Red Tape

If there is one thing that CIOs hate it's **red tape – bureaucratic roadblocks** that keep the IT department from doing what it is supposed to be doing. The very definition of information technology is that it moves fast and adapts to dynamic situations – exactly what a company's bureaucratic processes and barriers to success seem to be designed to prevent.

What CIOs need is a good role model for how to make this problem go away, it turns out that an American car company may be just the one to provide this...

A Little Bit Of History About General Motors...

General Motors is a really, really big company. General Motors is the world's largest manufacture of cars – Toyota is a close #2, but GM is still #1. Just like with every other large company, over the years **red tape as crept into GM processes** and this is now a significant problem.

Today GM has what others have called **a "plodding culture"**. This was never a good thing, but as a result of the recent global financial crisis it is something that can no longer be tolerated. When the financial crisis hit, GM was forced into bankruptcy. Only now are they starting to emerge from that financial situation. This means that they need to start to deliver on a host of new projects.

Although as CIO your firm may not have recently been in bankruptcy, your IT department and the IT sector as a whole certainly **has been on hold** for the last 1-2 years due to economic issues. Just like at GM, as we all start to get back to competing with the rest of the world, it is the CIO's responsibility to remove bureaucratic roadblocks and eliminate any lumbering processes that may be in place.

How GM Is Getting Rid Of Its Red Tape

If we can all agree that this is what needs to be done, then it all comes back to the million-dollar question: **what do we need to do to make it happen?** The good news for CIOs is that there is no magic involved; the bad news is that it just takes good old-fashioned hard work.

Ultimately what red tape does in any company is to **slow things down** and prevent new ideas from making it from the front lines where they are born to the upper levels of management where they can be implemented. Despite the importance of information technology, the IT department can face red tape issues just like the rest of the company.

Over at GM what they are doing to eliminate their red tape problem is to **put the right managers into the right roles**. It's important that the people that the CIO selects for these types of jobs not be afraid to speak their minds – this is how the existing red tape can be overcome.

These "change agents" within the IT department will have to do what is being done over at GM: **go out and be among the front line workers**. There will always be too many workers and too few change agents so what the change agents need to do is to act as cheerleaders for the IT workers. They need to encourage them to speak up and overcome the red tape that may be holding them back.

This involves making sure that when a worker identifies a new idea that they **speak up** and make sure that it gets brought to the attention of senior management. Likewise, when a project clearly becomes obsolete or will no longer serve its original purpose, IT department workers need to be encouraged to speak up and let others know that money, time, and effort is being wasted.

What All Of This Means For You

General Motors is a huge company with a long and checkered history – they've done some great stuff, but they've also **made a lot of mistakes**. We who work in the IT sector need to take the time to learn from them how they are working to eliminate the red tape that they have in their organization.

GM has all of the same problems that our companies have. Great ideas at the lower levels in the company **have a hard time** finding their way up to the decision makers who could decide to implement them. GM has a history of spending time and effort on projects that everyone knew would never see the light of day and they kept doing so because nobody spoke up.

In order to cut through all of their red tape, GM has placed **change agents** in charge of their new projects. These people have been given the assignment to create new projects that will get GM back on track. These "red tape cutters" are teaching the GM staff how to get their ideas through the red tape so that they can be considered and potentially cause changes to be made.

CIOs need to learn from the work that GM is doing. The importance of information technology is so great for companies that it's the job of the CIO to **make sure that nothing, including red tape, stands in the way of your next IT project**.

Chapter 12

How CIOs Work With Their Board Of Directors

Chapter 12: How CIOs Work With Their Board Of Directors

Congratulations CIO – you've been asked to **make a presentation** to your company's board of directors. Oh, oh. What are you going to have to do in order to make your career move forward due to this opportunity and not screw it up?

What Does A Board Of Directors Want From A CIO?

First off, let's all make sure that we're on the same page here – do you know exactly what your company's Board Of Directors is? It turns out that when you legally set up a company, you need to create a Board of Directors **to run the thing**. One of their first tasks is to find a CEO to run the day-to-day company. That's right – your CEO works for the Board of Directors. It really doesn't get any higher than this!

Although the Board does understand the importance of information technology, **they really don't care about the IT department** – they have much bigger things to worry about. That means that you are going to have present the information that they have requested very carefully.

Arthur Langer has done some research in this area and he has the following **four recommendations** for how CIOs should present information to their Board of Directors:

- **New Ideas:** CIOs need to understand why they have been asked to make a presentation to the Board. The Board is not interested in what you spend most of your time worrying about – budget details, hiring issues, etc. Instead, their focus is on the company as a whole and they want to hear from you what you can do to help the company grow. This can include how IT can help out with ongoing operations as well as what you can do more strategically.

- **Security:** Every presentation that a CIO makes to the Board needs to touch on the topic of information security. Remember, they don't care about the details. Instead, what they want to hear from you is what you are doing to protect the company against risks and what you are doing to ensure that the company's confidential information won't get stolen.

- **Data:** If there is one thing that is keeping your Board up at night, it's worrying about all of that data that your company is sitting on. As the CIO, they see you as being responsible for keeping track of all of this data. That also means that you are viewed as acting as the point-of-contact if the company gets sued and one of those e-discovery programs has to be conducted.

- **Analytics:** Since the Board sees the CIO as being in charge of all of the data that the company collects, they also see you as being responsible for finding ways to get the most out of that data. This means that you need to be ready to tell them how you plan on going about doing this.

How Can You Prepare For A Board Presentation?

Being invited to make a presentation to your company's board is a great honor. Now you're going to have to ensure that you **make the most of this opportunity**. That means, sorry about this, you're going to have to do some homework.

Here are **four things** that every CIO needs to do both before and during their presentation to the Board:

- **Know Your Audience:** You should do this before every presentation, and presenting to your Board is no different. You need to understand the personalities of the people who make up the Board. What is their background? What is their reputation within the company? What do other people who have presented to them have to say about them?

- **Make Friends:** How the presentation is going to turn out is often determined before it starts. If you can make contact with Board members before the day of the presentation and ask them questions, then you will have a chance to have an ally in your corner on the day of your presentation.

- **Time Counts:** When you were told how much time you had for your presentation, the person who told it to you was lying. The way that these things work out is that you never get as much time as you were told, or even as much as you ended up being allocated. The Board will hate you forever if you run over your allocated time and will love you forever if you finish up early. Always show up with multiple versions of your presentation so that you can present the version that will allow you to fit into smaller and smaller time periods.

- **Use Stories:** As the company's CIO you have a great deal of sophisticated knowledge about all things related to the IT sector and how they work. Don't share this during your presentation. Instead, keep things simple and use stories to make your points – this is what the Board will be able to remember.

What All Of This Means For You

The definition of information technology is that it is how a company uses computers to become more successful. As the company's CIO, it's your job to make this happen. When your Board summons you to present to them, you need to understand both **what they are interested in** and what they don't want you to talk about.

When you are preparing for your presentation you'll want to focus on **what the Board wants hear**: how IT can help to grow the company, data security, data management, and how best to use the data that the company has. Additionally you'll need to do your homework in order to prepare for your big presentation.

We talk a lot about finding ways to get the CIO **a "seat at the table"** when it comes to mapping out the company's future. Being asked to present to your Board is a fantastic opportunity for a CIO to make a name for himself or herself. Make sure that you take the time to prepare for this presentation and you'll see your career take off...

It's from the forge of failure that the steel of success is formed.

Hard Work Does Not Guarantee Success, But Success Does Not Happen Without Hard Work.

- Dr. Jim Anderson

Create IT Departments That Are Productive And A Valuable Asset To The Rest Of The Company !

Dr. Jim Anderson is available to provide training and coaching on the topics that are the most important to people who have to manage IT departments: how can I build a productive IT department (and keep it together) while at the same time providing the rest of the company with the IT services that they need?

Dr. Anderson believes that in order to both learn and remember what he says, speakers need to laugh. Each one of his speeches is full of fun and humor so that what he says "sticks" with everyone.

Dr. Anderson's CIO SkillsTraining Includes:

4. How to identify and attract the right type of IT workers to your IT department.
5. How to build relationships with the company's senior management in order to get the support that you need?
6. How to stay on top of changing technology and security issues so that you never get surprised?

Dr. Jim Anderson works with over 100 customers per year. To invite Dr. Anderson to work with you, contact him at:

Phone: 813-418-6970 or
Email: jim@BlueElephantConsulting.com

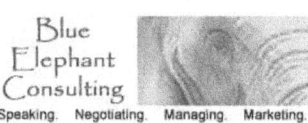

Photo Credits:

Cover - By: val.pearl
http://www.flickr.com/photos/valpearl/

Chapter 1 - By: Brian Carson
http://www.flickr.com/photos/thelearningcurvedotca/

Chapter 2 - By: David Feng
http://www.flickr.com/photos/fenng/

Chapter 3 - By: gillian maniscalco
http://www.flickr.com/photos/gillian_m/

Chapter 4 - By: Andy Melton
http://www.flickr.com/photos/trekkyandy/

Chapter 5 - By: Steve Garfield
http://www.flickr.com/photos/stevegarfield/

Chapter 6 - By: Kellogg School Of Management
http://www.kellogg.northwestern.edu/student/sp_event/marketing/

Chapter 7 - By: ROBERT HUFFSTUTTER
http://www.flickr.com/photos/huffstutterrobertl/

Chapter 8 - By: Steve Garfield
http://www.flickr.com/photos/stevegarfield/

Chapter 9 - By: rob Patrick
http://www.flickr.com/photos/alkalinezoo/

Chapter 10 - By: fabi42
http://www.flickr.com/photos/fabi42/

Chapter 11 - By: Frazgo
http://www.flickr.com/photos/frazgo/

Chapter 12 - By: Eric Dan
http://www.flickr.com/photos/ericphoto2/

Tips And Techniques For CIOs To Use In Order To Become Better Communicators

> This book has been written with one goal in mind – to show you how you can become a CIO who communicates clearly. It's not easy being a CIO so we're going to show you what you need to be doing in order to sure that everyone understands what needs to be done!
>
> **Let's Make Your CIO Career A Success!**

What You'll Find Inside:

- **FORGOTTEN IT SKILLS: HOW TO ASK QUESTIONS**

- **CIOS ASK THE QUESTION: IS TWITTER A FRIEND OR A FOE?**

- **SHOULD A CIO BOTHER WITH THAT ITIL STUFF?**

- **3 SKILLS THAT MOST CIOS ARE MISSING**

Dr. Jim Anderson brings his 25 years of real-world experience to this book. He's been a senior IT executive at some of the world's largest firms. He's going to show you what you need to do (and not do!) in order to make your CIO career a success!

www.ingramcontent.com/pod-product-compliance
Lightning Source LLC
Chambersburg PA
CBHW071810170526
45167CB00003B/1254